Big Houses

pieced by Donna Arends Hansen
quilted by Susan Corbett

These stately homes are appropriately bordered by open green spaces with plenty of parking for those special occasions that bring the entire family together for celebrating and memory making.

Large blocks go together quickly, for a fast, fun afternoon. This easy project is great for beginners.

instructions on pages 8 - 13

4 Striking Quilts to Make with Your Scraps, 'Jelly Rolls' or 2$\frac{1}{2}$" Strips

Big Houses
pages 4 - 5

Star Struck
pages 6 - 7

Tapestry
pages 32 - 33

Garden Lattice
pages 34 - 35

Star Struck

pieced by Donna Perrotta
quilted by Julie Lawson

Since early man gazed in awe upon the star-studded sky, connecting the points of light to form the patterns of the constellations, people have been making designs using stars. Now you can dream beneath a galaxy of your own making with this striking quilt.

Change the color of the stars to match your bedroom, or make a galaxy of different colors. The possibilities are as limitless as the night sky with this versatile design.

instructions on pages 14 - 17

Big Houses

Throw quilt size: 52" x 70"

Multiple Sizes

Need a larger quilt?

The quilts in this book are made as a throw-size quilt that uses 1 each of Black and 1 each of White 'Jelly Roll' fabrics, plus the addition of color fabrics.

All of the patterns in this book are made of components that can easily be repeated and sewn into larger quilts.

You will need to add additional fabrics for these larger quilts. Normally - double the fabric required for a twin, and triple the fabric required for a queen or king size bed quilt.

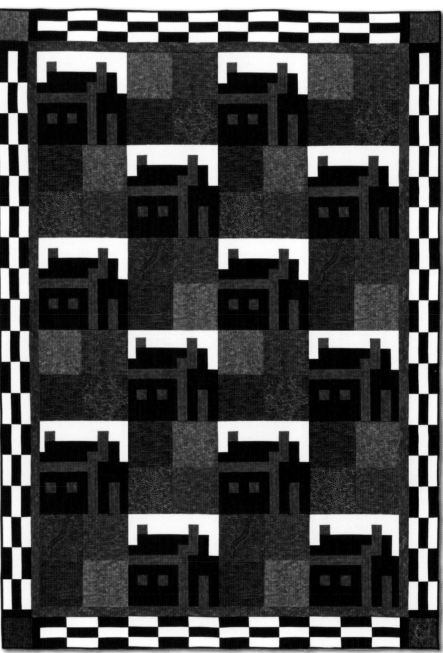

Big Houses

Double size quilt:
88" x 124"

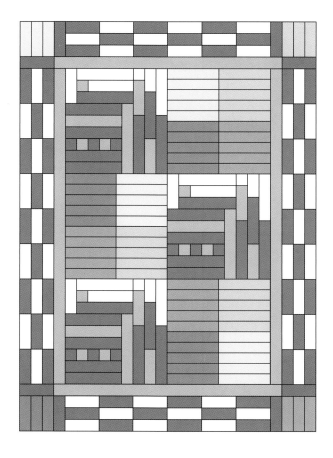

Big Houses

photos are on pages 4 - 5

SIZE: 52" x 70"

YARDAGE:
We used a *Moda* "Basics" Black and a "Basics" White
    'Jelly Roll' collection of $2\frac{1}{2}$" fabric strips.
    - we purchased 1 Black and 1 White 'Jelly Roll'
| 21 strips | OR | $1\frac{1}{2}$ yards Color A - White |
| 19 strips | OR | $1\frac{1}{3}$ yards Color B - Black |

We used a *Moda* "Marbles Bright"
    'Jelly Roll' collection of $2\frac{1}{2}$" fabric strips
    - we purchased 1 'Jelly Roll'
4 strips	OR	$\frac{1}{3}$ yard Color C - Red
4 strips	OR	$\frac{1}{3}$ yard Color D - Burgundy
4 strips	OR	$\frac{1}{3}$ yard Color E - Green
4 strips	OR	$\frac{1}{3}$ yard Color F - Forest Green
4 strips	OR	$\frac{1}{3}$ yard Color G - Royal Blue
4 strips	OR	$\frac{1}{3}$ yard Color H - Navy Blue

Backing	Purchase $3\frac{1}{4}$ yards
Batting	Purchase 60" x 78"
Binding	Purchase $\frac{1}{2}$ yard
Sewing machine, needle, thread	

FABRIC FOR INDIVIDUAL BLOCKS:
Sort the fabric colors as indicated.

Fabric for 1 Big House Block A:
Sort fabric for 3 House Blocks A.
1 strip	OR	$2\frac{1}{2}$" x 41" of Color A - White
1 strip	OR	$2\frac{1}{2}$" x $43\frac{1}{2}$" of Color C - Red
2 strips	OR	$2\frac{1}{2}$" x $89\frac{1}{2}$" of Color B - Black

Fabric for 1 Alternate Block B:
Sort fabric for 3 Alternate Blocks B.
2 strips	OR	$2\frac{1}{2}$" x $47\frac{1}{2}$" of Color E - Green
2 strips	OR	$2\frac{1}{2}$" x $47\frac{1}{2}$" of Color F - Forest Green
2 strips	OR	$2\frac{1}{2}$" x $47\frac{1}{2}$" of Color G - Royal Blue
2 strips	OR	$2\frac{1}{2}$" x $47\frac{1}{2}$" of Color H - Navy Blue

PREPARATION FOR STRIPS:
Cut all strips $2\frac{1}{2}$" by the width of fabric (usually 42" - 44").
Label the stacks or pieces as you cut.

Big House Block - A
CUTTING CHART

Quantity	Length	Position
Color A- White		
3	$10\frac{1}{2}$"	#3
6	$8\frac{1}{2}$"	#2, 12
3	$6\frac{1}{2}$"	#5
3	$4\frac{1}{2}$"	#9
3	$2\frac{1}{2}$"	#6
Color B - Black		
2	$31\frac{1}{2}$"	Unit 1-A
2	$31\frac{1}{2}$"	Unit 1-C
9	$10\frac{1}{2}$"	#4, 8, 13
3	$8\frac{1}{2}$"	#10
3	$7\frac{1}{2}$"	Unit 1-B
Color C - Red		
1	$31\frac{1}{2}$"	Unit 1-A
3	$12\frac{1}{2}$"	Unit 1
2	$7\frac{1}{2}$"	Unit 1-B
6	$6\frac{1}{2}$"	#7, 11
3	$2\frac{1}{2}$"	#1

SEW BLOCKS:
Refer to the Cutting Chart and Assembly instructions for
    each block.
Label the pieces as you cut.

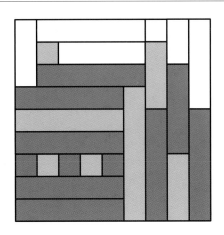

Big House Block - A

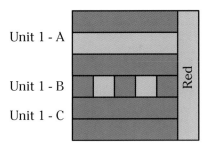

Unit 1 - A

Unit 1 - B

Unit 1 - C

Red

Unit 1 Assembly:
Sew Units A-B-C to make a piece $10\frac{1}{2}$" x $12\frac{1}{2}$". Press.
Sew a Red $2\frac{1}{2}$" x $12\frac{1}{2}$" strip to the right side of the piece. Press.
Make 3 of Unit 1.

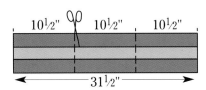

$10\frac{1}{2}$" $10\frac{1}{2}$" $10\frac{1}{2}$"

$31\frac{1}{2}$"

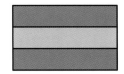

Unit 1 - A

Unit 1 - A:
Sew 3 Unit 1 - A strips together B-R-B to make a piece
$6\frac{1}{2}$" x $31\frac{1}{2}$". Press.
Cut the piece into 3 sections $6\frac{1}{2}$" x $10\frac{1}{2}$".
Label them Unit 1-A.

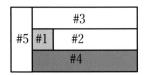

#3
#5 #1 #2
#4

Unit 2

Unit 2:
Sew #1-2. Press.
Sew #3 & 4 to the top and
bottom of the piece. Press.
Sew #5 to the left side of the
piece. Press.
Make 3.

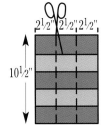

$2\frac{1}{2}$" $2\frac{1}{2}$" $2\frac{1}{2}$"

$10\frac{1}{2}$"

Unit 1 - B

Unit 1 - B:
Sew 5 Unit 1 - B strips together B-R-B-R-B to make a piece
$7\frac{1}{2}$" x $10\frac{1}{2}$". Press.
Cut the piece into 3 sections $2\frac{1}{2}$" x $10\frac{1}{2}$".
Label them Unit 1-B.

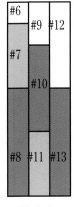

#6
#9 #12
#7
#10
#8 #11 #13

Unit 3

Unit 3: .
Column 1: Sew #6-7-8. Press.
Column 2: Sew #9-10-11. Press.
Column 3: Sew #12-13. Press.
Sew the columns together. Press.
Make 3.

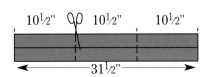

$10\frac{1}{2}$" $10\frac{1}{2}$" $10\frac{1}{2}$"

$31\frac{1}{2}$"

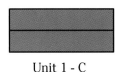

Unit 1 - C

Unit 1 - C:
Sew 2 Unit 1 - C strips together B-B to make a piece
$4\frac{1}{2}$" x $31\frac{1}{2}$". Press.
Cut the piece into 3 sections $4\frac{1}{2}$" x $10\frac{1}{2}$".
Label them Unit 1-C.

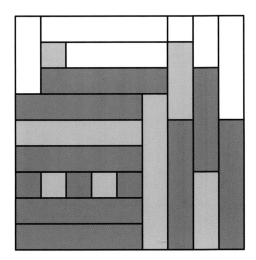

Big House Block Finished

Big House Block A Assembly:
Sew Unit 1-2. Press.
Sew Unit 3 to the right side of the piece. Press.
The block will measure $18\frac{1}{2}$" x $18\frac{1}{2}$".
Make 3 Big House blocks.

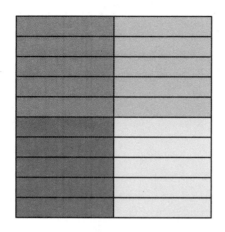

Alternate Block - B

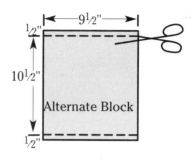

Trim Each Block:
Trim each block to $9\frac{1}{2}$" x $9\frac{1}{2}$" by cutting $\frac{1}{2}$" off the top and bottom of each square.

Alternate Blocks - B

CUTTING CHART

	Quantity	Length
Color E - Green		
	5	$28\frac{1}{2}$"
Color F - Forest Green		
	5	$28\frac{1}{2}$"
Color G - Royal Blue		
	5	$28\frac{1}{2}$"
Color H - Navy Blue		
	5	$28\frac{1}{2}$"

Use these strips to make 3 Alternate blocks of each color.

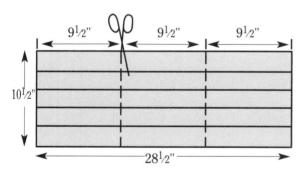

Sew strips together and cut 3 pieces.

Squares for Alternate Blocks:
Refer to the Block B diagram.

Make 3 of each square.
> Sew 5 Green $28\frac{1}{2}$" strips together to make a piece $10\frac{1}{2}$" x $28\frac{1}{2}$". Press.
> Cut the strip-set into 3 pieces, each $9\frac{1}{2}$" x $10\frac{1}{2}$".

> Repeat for Royal Blue strips.
> Repeat for Navy Blue strips.
> Repeat for Forest Green strips.

Alternate Block Assembly:
Refer to the color placement in each row.
> Sew the squares together in 2 rows,
> 2 squares per row. Press.
> The block will measure $18\frac{1}{2}$" x $18\frac{1}{2}$".

Make 3 Alternate blocks.

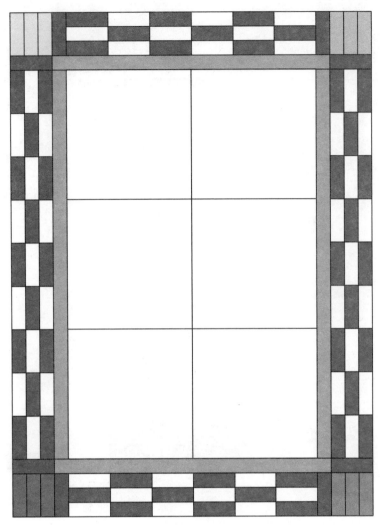

Big Houses
Borders Assembly Diagram

ASSEMBLY:

Refer to the Quilt Assembly diagram on page 13.

Arrange all blocks on a work surface or table.

Rows 1 & 3:
Sew a House block to an Alternate Block. Press.

Row 2:
Sew an Alternate Block to a House block. Press.

Assembly:
Sew the 3 rows together. Press.

BORDERS:

Border #1:

Sew 4 Burgundy strips and any leftover Red strips together (alternating the colors) end to end so you will have enough fabric.

Cut 2 strips $2\frac{1}{2}$" x $54\frac{1}{2}$" for sides.
Cut 2 strips $2\frac{1}{2}$" x $40\frac{1}{2}$" for top and bottom.
Sew side borders to the quilt. Press.
Sew top and bottom borders to the quilt. Press.

Pieced Border #2:

Cornerstones C:

From Green, Royal Blue, Navy Blue, and Forest Green, cut 3 strips $6\frac{1}{2}$" long.

For each color, sew 3 strips together to make a square $6\frac{1}{2}$" x $6\frac{1}{2}$". Press.

Label the Green C - 1, Royal Blue C - 2, Navy Blue C - 3, and Forest Green C - 4.

Strip D:

Cut 8 Black strips $2\frac{1}{2}$" x $6\frac{1}{2}$".

Cutting for Blocks A & B:

Cut 6 Black and 6 White strips 39" long for Blocks A & B.
Cut 1 White and 2 Black strips 26" long for Block A.
Cut 1 Black and 2 White strips 13" long for Block B.
Refer to the Border #2 Diagrams.

Block A:

Sew 39" strips together B-W-B. Press. Make 2.
Sew 26" strips together B-W-B. Press.
Cut 16 squares $6\frac{1}{2}$" x $6\frac{1}{2}$".

Block B:

Sew 39" strips together W-B-W. Press. Make 2.
Sew 13" strips together W-B-W. Press.
Cut 14 squares $6\frac{1}{2}$" x $6\frac{1}{2}$".

Side Borders:

Sew A-B-A-B-A-B-A-B-A. Press. Make 2.
Sew a strip D to each end of each side border.
Sew side borders to the quilt. Press.

Top and Bottom Borders:

Sew A-B-A-B-A-B. Press. Make 2.
Sew a strip D to each end of each border. Press.
Sew a Cornerstone to each end of each border. Press.
Sew borders to the top and bottom of the quilt. Press.

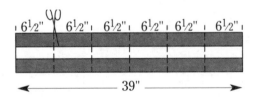

$6\frac{1}{2}$" $6\frac{1}{2}$" $6\frac{1}{2}$" $6\frac{1}{2}$" $6\frac{1}{2}$" $6\frac{1}{2}$"

← 39" →

Border #2 - Block A
Make 2 sets of 39" strips.
Make 1 set of 26" strips.

Cut 16 squares $6\frac{1}{2}$" x $6\frac{1}{2}$".

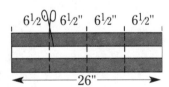

$6\frac{1}{2}$ $6\frac{1}{2}$" $6\frac{1}{2}$" $6\frac{1}{2}$"

← 26" →

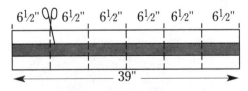

$6\frac{1}{2}$" $6\frac{1}{2}$" $6\frac{1}{2}$" $6\frac{1}{2}$" $6\frac{1}{2}$" $6\frac{1}{2}$"

← 39" →

Border #2 - Block B
Make 2 sets of 39" strips.
Make 1 set of 13" strips.

Cut 14 squares $6\frac{1}{2}$" x $6\frac{1}{2}$".

$6\frac{1}{2}$" $6\frac{1}{2}$"

← 13" →

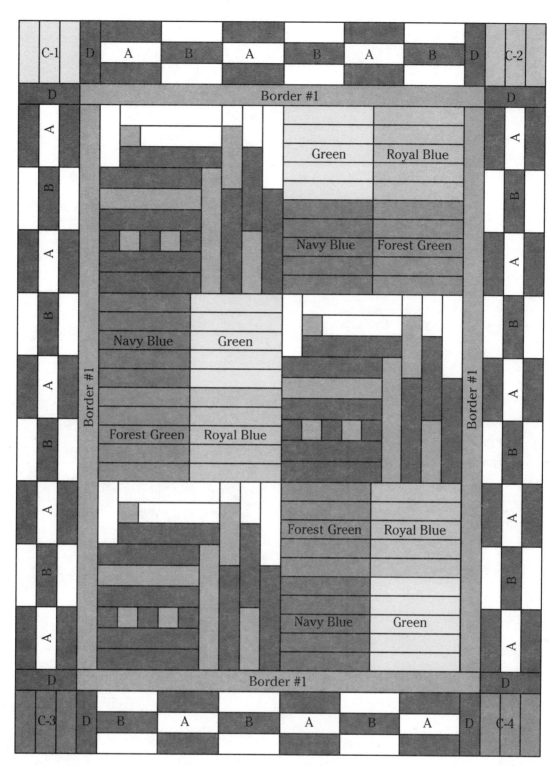

Big Houses Finished
Assembly Diagram

FINISHING:
Quilting:
 See Basic Instructions.

Binding:
 Cut strips 2½" wide.
 Sew together end to end to equal 254".
 See Binding Instructions.

Star Struck

photos are on pages 6 - 7

SIZE: 52" x 68"

YARDAGE:
We used a *Moda* "Basics" Black and a "Basics" White
   'Jelly Roll' collection of $2\frac{1}{2}$" fabric strips.
   - we purchased 1 Black and 1 White 'Jelly Roll'

25 strips	OR	$1\frac{7}{8}$ yards Color A - White
25 strips	OR	$1\frac{7}{8}$ yards Color B - Black

We used a *Moda* "Marbles Bright"
   'Jelly Roll' collection of $2\frac{1}{2}$" fabric strips
   - we purchased 1 'Jelly Roll'

3 strips	OR	$\frac{1}{4}$ yard Color C - Light Blue
4 strips	OR	$\frac{1}{3}$ yard Color D - Green
3 strips	OR	$\frac{1}{4}$ yard Color E - Red
4 strips	OR	$\frac{1}{3}$ yard Color F - Dark Blue
Backing		Purchase $3\frac{1}{8}$ yards
Batting		Purchase 60" x 76"

Sewing machine, needle, thread
Optional: EZ 'Easy Star & Geese' Templates makes cutting
   flying geese and triangles easier

FABRIC FOR ONE BLOCK:

Fabric or Scraps for 1 Star Block:

1 strip	OR	$2\frac{1}{2}$" x 28" of Color A - White
1 strip	OR	$2\frac{1}{2}$" x 29" of Red, Blue, Lt Blue or Green

Fabric or Scraps for 1 Alternate Block:

1 strip	OR	$2\frac{1}{2}$" x 18" of Color A - White
1 strip	OR	$2\frac{1}{2}$" x 19" of Color B - Black

PREPARATION FOR STRIPS:
   Cut all strips $2\frac{1}{2}$" by the width of fabric (usually 42" - 44").
   Label the stacks or pieces as you cut.

CUTTING CHART

Quantity	Length	Position
Color A - White		
4	42"	Alternate Block - Center
34	$4\frac{1}{2}$"	Alternate Block - Rows 1 & 3
72	$4\frac{1}{2}$"	Star Block background
72	$2\frac{1}{2}$"	Star Block - Rows 1 & 3
Color B - Black		
4	42"	Alternate Block - Center
68	$2\frac{1}{2}$"	Alternate Block - Rows 1 & 3
Color C - Light Blue		
2	18"	Star Block - Centers
32	$2\frac{1}{2}$"	Star Points
Color D - Green		
2	$22\frac{1}{2}$"	Star Block - Centers
40	$2\frac{1}{2}$"	Star Points
Color E - Red		
2	18"	Star Block - Centers
32	$2\frac{1}{2}$"	Star Points
Color F - Dark Blue		
2	$22\frac{1}{2}$"	Star Block - Centers
40	$2\frac{1}{2}$"	Star Points

Alternate Block

MAKE THE BLOCKS:
Alternate Blocks:
   Make a total of 17 blocks.

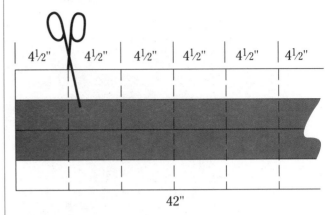

42"

Block Center:
   Sew 42" strips together W-B-B-W to make a piece
     $8\frac{1}{2}$" x 42". Press.
   Make 2 sets.
   Cut 17 sections, each $4\frac{1}{2}$" x $8\frac{1}{2}$". Press.

Block Center:
   Cut a total of 17 units $4\frac{1}{2}$" x $8\frac{1}{2}$". Press.

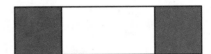

Rows 1 & 3:
   Sew a Black square on each end of a White
     $2\frac{1}{2}$" x $4\frac{1}{2}$" strip. Press.
   Make a total of 34 units.

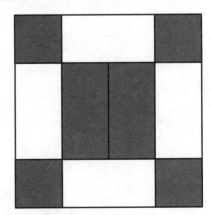

Alternate Block Assembly Diagram

Block Assembly:.
   Sew the rows together. Press.
   Make a total of 17 Alternate blocks.

Star Block

MAKE THE BLOCKS:
Star Blocks:
>   Make a total of 18 blocks:
>   4 Red
>   4 Light Blue,
>   5 Green
>   5 Dark Blue

 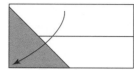

Align a square with the end of the block.
Sew a diagonal line. Fold back the triangle. Press.

Align a square with the other end of the block.
Sew a diagonal line. Fold back the triangle. Press.

Flying Geese Assembly

Flying Geese Sections:
>   Make 4 for each block for a total of 72 sections.
>   Align the colored square with the end of the
>   White 2½" x 4½" background strip.
>   Sew on the diagonal and fold back. Press.
>   Repeat for the other end of the strip.

Red & Light Blue - Star Centers
>   Sew 2 strips 18" long together to make a strip-set
>   4½" wide. Press.
>   Cut 4 squares 4½" x 4½".

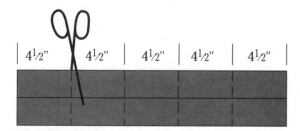

Green & Dark Blue - Star Centers
>   Sew 2 strips 22½" long together to make a strip-set
>   4½" wide. Press.
>   Cut 5 squares 4½" x 4½".

 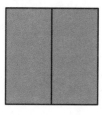

Star Center

Star Center:
>   Cut the following 4½" x 4½" squares:
>   4 Red
>   4 Light Blue
>   5 Green
>   5 Dark Blue

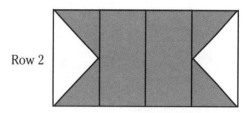

Row 2

Row 2:
>   Sew a Flying Geese section (in a matching color)
>   to the right and left sides of each colored
>   4½" x 4½" square. Press.

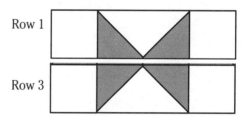

Row 1

Row 3

Rows 1 & 3:
>   Sew a White 2½" x 2½" square on each end of
>   2 Flying Geese sections. Press.

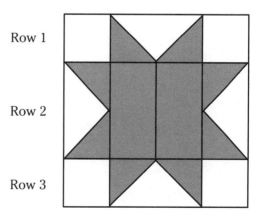

Row 1

Row 2

Row 3

Star Block Assembly Diagram

Star Block Assembly:
>   Sew the rows together. Press.
>   Make a total of 18 Star blocks:
>   4 Light Blue
>   4 Red
>   5 Green
>   5 Dark Blue

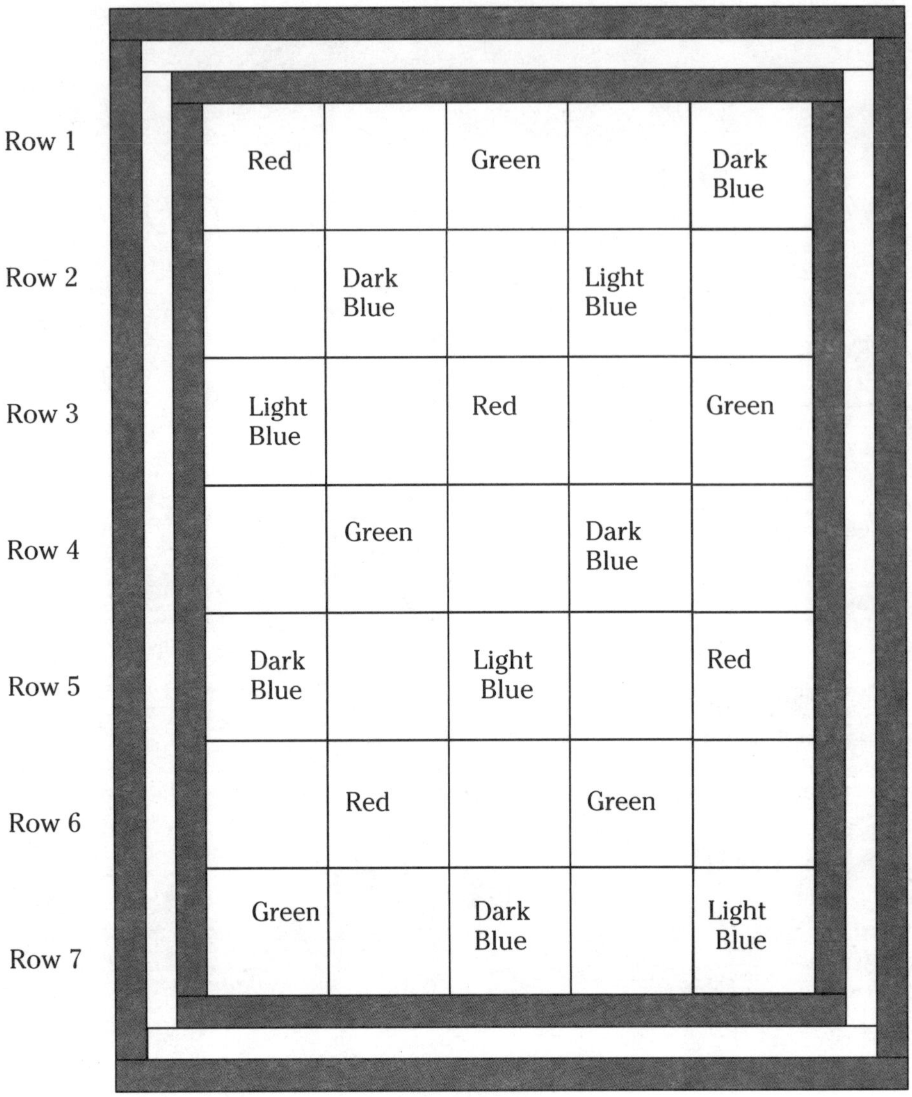

	Row	Col 1	Col 2	Col 3	Col 4	Col 5
Row 1		Red		Green		Dark Blue
Row 2			Dark Blue		Light Blue	
Row 3		Light Blue		Red		Green
Row 4			Green		Dark Blue	
Row 5		Dark Blue		Light Blue		Red
Row 6			Red		Green	
Row 7		Green		Dark Blue		Light Blue

Star Struck Quilt
Assembly Diagram

QUILT ASSEMBLY:

Refer to the Quilt Assembly diagram.
Arrange all blocks on a work surface or table.

Sew blocks together in rows, with 5 blocks
on each row. Press.

Sew the 7 rows together. Press.

BORDERS:

Border #1:
Use 5 strips of Fabric B - Black. Sew strips together end to end.
Cut 2 strips $2\frac{1}{2}$" x $56\frac{1}{2}$" for sides.
Cut 2 strips $2\frac{1}{2}$" x $44\frac{1}{2}$" for top and bottom.
Sew side borders to the quilt. Press.
Sew top and bottom borders to the quilt. Press.

Border #2:
Use 6 strips of Fabric A - White. Sew strips together end to end.
Cut 2 strips $2\frac{1}{2}$" x $60\frac{1}{2}$" for sides.
Cut 2 strips $2\frac{1}{2}$" x $48\frac{1}{2}$" for top and bottom.
Sew side borders to the quilt. Press.
Sew top and bottom borders to the quilt. Press.

Border #3:
Use 6 strips of Fabric B - Black. Sew strips together end to end.
Cut 2 strips $2\frac{1}{2}$" x $64\frac{1}{2}$" for sides.
Cut 2 strips $2\frac{1}{2}$" x $52\frac{1}{2}$" for top and bottom.
Sew side borders to the quilt. Press.
Sew top and bottom borders to the quilt. Press.

Star Struck
Finished Quilt Assembly Diagram

FINISHING:
Quilting:
    See Basic Instructions.

Binding:
    Cut strips $2\frac{1}{2}$" wide.
    Sew together end to end to equal 250".
    See Binding Instructions.

The Best Things About 'Jelly Rolls'

I love to quilt, but it is often difficult to find time to cut and piece a quilt top. When I saw collections of 2½" pre-cut fabric strips, I knew they were the answer.

No more spending hours choosing and cutting fabrics. Now I can begin sewing right away. Beautiful colors are available in every set. So whether I like jewel colors, heritage patterns, soft pastels or earthy tones... there is an assortment for me.

Now my goals... a handmade cover for every bed, an heirloom quilt for each new baby and a pieced quilt for each of my children... are within reach. With 'Jelly Rolls' it is possible to complete a quilt top in a weekend.

After I piece all the blocks together, I use leftover strips for the borders and binding. Nothing really goes to waste and, if needed, I can purchase a bit of extra fabric for an extra punch of color or an additional yard for the border.

TIP: Quantities are given in strips and yardage so you know what you need and can start right away.

Tips for Working with Strips

Guide for Yardage:

2½" Strips - Each ¼ yard or a 'Fat Quarter' equals 3 strips - A pre-cut 'Jelly Roll' strip is 2½" x 44"

Pre-cut strips are cut on the crosswise grain and are prone to stretching. These tips will help reduce stretching and make your quilt lay flat for quilting.

1. If you are cutting yardage, cut on the grain. Cut fat quarters on grain, parallel to the 18" side.

2. When sewing crosswise grain strips together, take care not to stretch the strips. If you detect any puckering as you go, rip out the seam and sew it again.

3. Press, Do Not Iron. Carefully open fabric, with the seam to one side, press without moving the iron. A back-and-forth ironing motion stretches the fabric.

4. Reduce the wiggle in your borders with this technique from garment making. First, accurately cut your borders to the exact measure of the quilt top. Then, before sewing the border to the quilt, run a double row of stay stitches along the outside edge to maintain the original shape and prevent stretching. Pin the border to the quilt, taking care not to stretch the quilt top to make it fit. Pinning reduces slipping and stretching.

Rotary Cutting

Rotary Cutter: Friend or Foe

A rotary cutter is wonderful and useful. When not used correctly, the sharp blade can be a dangerous tool. Follow these safety tips:

1. Never cut toward you.

2. Use a sharp blade. Pressing harder on a dull blade can cause the blade to jump the ruler and injure your fingers.

3. Always disengage the blade before the cutter leaves your hand, even if you intend to pick it up immediately.

Rotary cutters have been caught when lifting fabric, have fallen onto the floor and have cut fingers.

Basic Sewing

You now have precisely cut strips that are exactly the correct width. You are well on your way to blocks that fit together perfectly. Accurate sewing is the next important step.

Matching Edges:

1. Carefully line up the edges of your strips. Many times, if the underside is off a little, your seam will be off by $\frac{1}{8}$". This does not sound like much until you have 8 seams in a block, each off by $\frac{1}{8}$". Now your finished block is a whole inch wrong!

2. Pin the pieces together to prevent them shifting.

Seam Allowance:

I cannot stress enough the importance of accurate $\frac{1}{4}$" seams. All the quilts in this book are measured for $\frac{1}{4}$" seams unless otherwise indicated.

Most sewing machine manufacturers offer a Quarter-inch foot. A Quarter-inch foot is the most worthwhile investment you can make in your quilting.

Pressing:

I want to talk about pressing even before we get to sewing because proper pressing can make the difference between a quilt that wins a ribbon at the quilt show and one that does not.

Press, do NOT iron. What does that mean? Many of us want to move the iron back and forth along the seam. This "ironing" stretches the strip out of shape and creates errors that accumulate as the quilt is constructed. Believe it or not, there is a correct way to press your seams, and here it is:

1. Do NOT use steam with your iron. If you need a little water, spritz it on.

2. Place your fabric flat on the ironing board without opening the seam. Set a hot iron on the seam and count to 3. Lift the iron and move to the next position along the seam. Repeat until the entire seam is pressed. This sets and sinks the threads into the fabric.

3. Now, carefully lift the top strip and fold it away from you so the seam is on one side. Usually the seam is pressed toward the darker fabric, but often the direction of the seam is determined by the piecing requirements.

4. Press the seam open with your fingers. Add a little water or spray starch if it wants to close again. Lift the iron and place it on the seam. Count to 3. Lift the iron again and continue until the seam is pressed. Do NOT

use the tip of the iron to push the seam open. So many people do this and wonder later why their blocks are not fitting together.

5. Most critical of all: For accuracy every seam must be pressed before the next seam is sewn.

Working with 'Crosswise Grain' Strips:

Strips cut on the crosswise grain (from selvage to selvage) have problems similar to bias edges and are prone to stretching. To reduce stretching and make your quilt lay flat for quilting, keep these tips in mind.

1. Take care not to stretch the strips as you sew.

2. Adjust the sewing thread tension and the presser foot pressure if needed.

3. If you detect any puckering as you go, rip out the seam and sew it again. It is much easier to take out a seam now than to do it after the block is sewn.

Sewing Bias Edges:

Bias edges wiggle and stretch out of shape very easily. They are not recommended for beginners, but even a novice can accomplish bias edges if these techniques are employed.

1. Stabilize the bias edge with one of these methods:

a) Press with spray starch.

b) Press freezer paper or removable iron-on stabilizer to the back of the fabric.

c) Sew a double row of stay stitches along the bias edge and $\frac{1}{8}$" from the bias edge. This is a favorite technique of garment makers.

2. Pin, pin, pin! I know many of us dislike pinning, but when working with bias edges, pinning makes the difference between intersections that match and those that do not.

Building Better Borders:

Wiggly borders make a quilt very difficult to finish. However, wiggly borders can be avoided with these techniques.

1. Cut the borders on grain. That means cutting your strips parallel to the selvage edge.

2. Accurately cut your borders to the exact measure of the quilt.

3. If your borders are piece stripped from crosswise grain fabrics, press well with spray starch and sew a double row of stay stitches along the outside edge to maintain the original shape and prevent stretching.

4. Pin the border to the quilt, taking care not to stretch the quilt top to make it fit. Pinning reduces slipping and stretching.

Embroidery   Use 24" lengths of doubled pearl cotton or 6-ply floss and a #22 or #24 Chenille needle (this needle has a large eye). Outline large elements.

Running Stitch   Come up at A. Weave the needle through the fabric, making LONG stitches on the top and SHORT stitches on the bottom. Keep stitches even.

Applique Instructions

Basic Turned Edge

1. Trace pattern onto no-melt template plastic (or onto Wash-Away Tear-Away Stabilizer).

2. Cut out the fabric shape leaving a scant ¼" fabric border all around and clip the curves.

3. **Plastic Template Method -** Place plastic shape on the wrong side of the fabric. Spray edges with starch. Press a ¼" border over the edge of the template plastic with the tip of a hot iron. Press firmly.

4. **Stabilizer Method -** Place stabilizer shape on the wrong side of the fabric. Use a glue stick to press a ¼" border over the edge of the stabilizer securing it with the glue stick. Press firmly.

5. Remove the template, maintaining the folded edge on the back of the fabric.

6. Position the shape on the quilt and Blindstitch in place.

Basic Turned Edge by Hand

1. Cut out the shape leaving a ¼" fabric border all around.

2. Baste the shapes to the quilt, keeping the basting stitches away from the edge of the fabric.

3. Begin with all areas that are under other layers and work to the topmost layer.

4. For an area no more than 2" ahead of where you are working, trim to ⅛" and clip the curves.

5. Using the needle, roll the edge under and sew tiny Blindstitches to secure.

Using Fusible Web for Iron-on Applique:

1. Trace pattern onto Steam a Seam 2 fusible web.

2. Press the patterns onto the wrong side of fabric.

3. Cut out patterns exactly on the drawn line.

4. Score web paper with a pin, then remove the paper.

5. Position the fabric, fusible side down, on the quilt. Press with a hot iron following the fusible web manufacturer's instructions.

6. Stitch around the edge by hand.

Optional: Stabilize the wrong side of the fabric with your favorite stabilizer.

Use a size 80 machine embroidery needle. Fill the bobbin with lightweight basting thread and thread machine with machine embroidery thread that complements the color being appliqued.

Set your machine for a Zigzag stitch and adjust the thread tension if needed. Use a scrap to experiment with different stitch widths and lengths until you find the one you like best.

Sew slowly.

Basic Layering Instructions

Marking Your Quilt:

If you choose to mark your quilt for hand or machine quilting, it is much easier to do so before layering. Press your quilt before you begin. Here are some handy tips regarding marking.

1. A disappearing pen may vanish before you finish.

2. Use a White pencil on dark fabrics.

3. If using a washable Blue pen, remember that pressing may make the pen permanent.

Pieced Backings:

1. Press the backing fabric before measuring.

2. If possible cut backing fabrics on grain, parallel to the selvage edges.

3. Piece 3 parts rather than 2 whenever possible, sewing 2 side borders to the center. This reduces stress on the pieced seam.

4. Backing and batting should extend at least 2" on each side of the quilt.

Creating a Quilt Sandwich:

1. Press the backing and top to remove all wrinkles.

2. Lay the backing wrong side up on the table.

3. Position the batting over the backing and smooth out all wrinkles.

4. Center the quilt top over the batting leaving a 2" border all around.

5. Pin the layers together with 2" safety pins positioned a handwidth apart. A grapefruit spoon makes inserting the pins easier. Leaving the pins open in the container speeds up the basting on the next quilt.

Basic Quilting Instructions

Hand Quilting:

Many quilters enjoy the serenity of hand quilting. Because the quilt is handled a great deal, it is important to securely baste the sandwich together. Place the quilt in a hoop and don't forget to hide your knots.

Machine Quilting:

All the quilts in this book were machine quilted. Some were quilted on a large, free-arm quilting machine and others were quilted on a sewing machine. If you have never machine quilted before, practice on some scraps first.

Straight Line Machine Quilting Tips:

1. Pin baste the layers securely.

2. Set up your sewing machine with a size 80 quilting needle and a walking foot.

3. Experimenting with the decorative stitches on your machine adds interest to your quilt. You do not have to quilt the entire piece with the same stitch. Variety is the spice of life, so have fun trying out stitches you have never used before as well as your favorite stand-bys.

Free Motion Machine Quilting Tips:

1. Pin baste the layers securely.

2. Set up your sewing machine with a spring needle, a quilting foot, and lower the feed dogs.

Basic Mitered Binding

A Perfect Finish:

The binding endures the most stress on a quilt and is usually the first thing to wear out. For this reason, we recommend using a double fold binding.

1. Trim the backing and batting even with the quilt edge.

2. If possible cut strips on the crosswise grain because a little bias in the binding is a Good thing. This is the only place in the quilt where bias is helpful, for it allows the binding to give as it is turned to the back and sewn in place.

3. Strips are usually cut 2½" wide, but check the instructions for your project before cutting.

4. Sew strips end to end to make a long strip sufficient to go all around the quilt plus 4"- 6".

5. With wrong sides together, fold the strip in half lengthwise. Press.

6. Stretch out your hand and place your little finger at the corner of the quilt top. Place the binding where your thumb touches the edge of the quilt. Aligning the edge of the quilt with the raw edges of the binding, pin the binding in place along the first side.

7. Leaving a 2" tail for later use, begin sewing the binding to the quilt with a ¼" seam.

For Mitered Corners:

1. Stop ¼" from the first corner. Leave the needle in the quilt and turn it 90°. Hit the reverse button on your machine and back off the quilt leaving the threads connected.

2. Fold the binding perpendicular to the side you sewed, making a 45° angle. Carefully maintaining the first fold, bring the binding back along the edge to be sewn.

3. Carefully align the edges of the binding with the quilt edge and sew as you did the first side. Repeat this process until you reach the tail left at the beginning. Fold the tail out of the way and sew until you are ¼" from the beginning stitches.

4. Remove the quilt from the machine. Fold the quilt out of the way and match the binding tails together. Carefully sew the binding tails with a ¼" seam. You can do this by hand if you prefer.

Finishing the Binding:

5. Trim the seam to reduce bulk.

6. Finish stitching the binding to the quilt across the join you just sewed.

7. Turn the binding to the back of the quilt. To reduce bulk at the corners, fold the miter in the opposite direction from which it was folded on the front.

8. Hand-sew a Blind stitch on the back of the quilt to secure the binding in place.

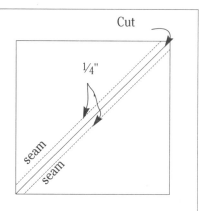

Half-Square Triangle

1. Place 2 squares right sides together.
2. Draw a diagonal line from corner to corner.
3. Stitch ¼" on each side of the line.
4. Cut squares apart on the diagonal line.
5. Open the 2 new squares with 2 colors.
6. Press. Trim off dog-ears.
7. Center and trim to size.

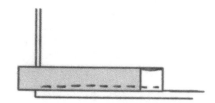

Align the raw edge of the binding with the raw edge of the quilt top. Start about 8" from the corner and go along the first side with a ¼" seam.

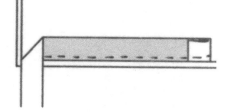

Stop ¼" from the edge. Then stitch a slant to the corner (through both layers of binding)... lift up, then down, as you line up the edge. Fold the binding back.

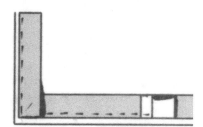

Align the raw edge again. Continue stitching the next side with a ¼" seam as you sew the binding in place.

Garden Lattice

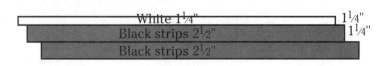

White 1¼"   1¼"
Black strips 2½"   1¼"
Black strips 2½"

photos are on pages 34 - 35.

SIZE: 46" x 66"

YARDAGE:

We used a *Moda* "Basics" Black and a "Basics" White
   'Jelly Roll' collections of 2½" fabric strips.
   - we purchased 1 Black and 1 White Jelly Roll

| 39 strips | OR | 2¾ yards Black |
| 16 strips | OR | 1⅙ yards White |

We also used a *Moda* "The Caroler" by Mary Engelbreit
   'Layer Cake' collection of 10" fabric squares.
   - we purchased 1 Layer Cake

Six 10" squares	OR	⅝ yard of Red print
Three 10" squares	OR	⅓ yard of Green print
One 10" square	OR	⅓ yard of Yellow print

Backing   Purchase 2¾ yards
Batting   Purchase 54" x 74"
Sewing machine, needle, thread

Optional: "A Girl's Best Friend" Diamond Cut
   template ruler by June Tailor.
   This plastic template makes cutting diamonds easy.

PREPARATION FOR STRIPS:
   Cut all Black strips 2½" x 44".
   Cut all White strips 2½" x 44".
   Tip: Do not remove the selvage edge before cutting the
diamonds. You need the entire 44". The selvage edge will
be removed with the first and last cuts.

SORTING:
   Sort the Black and White strips into stacks as you cut.
   Save the color squares for Applique flowers.

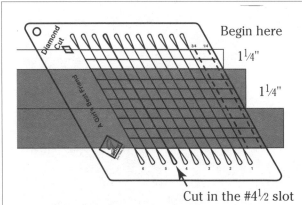

Begin here

1¼"

1¼"

Cut in the #4½ slot

Tips for Cutting with the Diamond Template -
   You will use the same cut mark slot for all diamonds.
   Align the bottom line of the template with the
edge of fabric strip-set bottom edge. Begin close to
the right edge of strips. Make one diagonal cut on the
right side to trim off the staggered ends.
   Now place a rotary cutter in the #4½ slot and
cut. You should have 1 diamond.
   Move template to realign the right edge. Place
rotary cutter in #4½ slot and cut again. You have 2
diamonds.
   Repeat along the strip-set to make 8 diamonds.

Make 61 Black Diamonds with White Sashing:
Cut the Strips:-
   You'll need 16 Black strips, each 2½" x 44".
   You'll need 8 White Sashing strips, each 1¼" x 44".

SEW STRIP-SETS:
   Sew the strips together side by side,
      White - Black - Black
   Be sure to stagger the strips from the **right side as shown**.
   Press.
   Make 8 strip-sets.

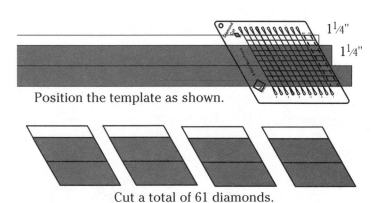

1¼"

1¼"

Position the template as shown.

Cut a total of 61 diamonds.

Cut Diamond Shapes:
   Cut each strip-set individually.
   Position the ruler as shown.
   Place the rotary cutter in the #4½ slot and cut.
   Cut a total of 61 diamonds.
      (Each 44" strip-set will yield 8 diamonds.)

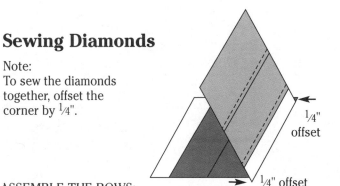

Sewing Diamonds

Note:
To sew the diamonds
together, offset the
corner by ¼".

¼"
offset

¼" offset

ASSEMBLE THE ROWS:
   Refer to diagram to the right for block placement.
   Arrange all blocks in diagonal rows on a work surface.
   Refer to the Sewing Diamonds diagram.
   When sewing diamonds together, offset the edge by ¼".
   Sew the diamonds for each row together.

Align Seams for Diamonds

Tips for Aligning Diamond Seams on Sashing:

If you have not sewn diamonds before, it can be a bit tricky to match the seams.

Refer to the diagrams.

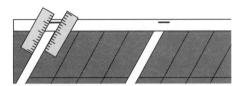

Align Sashing Seams

Step 1:

On the right side of the sashing, draw lines with a chalk marker $1/4$" from the outer edge.

Align rulers or a straight edge with the sashing seams.

Make dots extending from the intersections, $3/4$" apart.

You will insert pins at these dots.

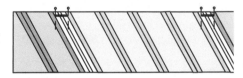

Step 2:

Position the pieced row on top of the sashing row, with right sides together.

Place pins $1/4$" from the outer fabric edge, aligning the marks with the short sashing seams.

Insert the pins through the dots you made in step 1.

QUILT ASSEMBLY:

Refer to the 'Align Seams for Diamonds' diagrams.

Pin and sew the rows together. Press.

PREPARE SASHING STRIPS:

TIP: Because of the angles involved, the lengths given are longer than needed. The excess will be trimmed when the center is squared up.

Cut Sashing Strips:

Sashing A - Cut 4 White strips $1/4$" x 22".

Sashing B - Cut 4 White strips $1/4$" x 44".

Sashing C - Cut 2 White strips $1/4$" x 66".

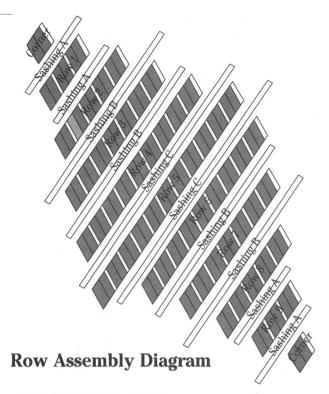

Row Assembly Diagram

SEW THE SASHING STRIPS:

Center and sew a 22" sashing to each side of row 1. Repeat for row 9. Press.

Center and sew 44" sashing to each side of row 3. Repeat for row 7. Press.

Center and sew 66" sashing to each side of row 5. Press.

QUILT ASSEMBLY:

Refer to the 'Align Seams for Diamonds' diagrams.

Pin and sew the rows together. Press.

Quilt Center

SQUARE UP THE QUILT CENTER:

Refer to the Quilt Center diagram.

Square up the quilt center to $26 1/2$" x $46 1/2$".

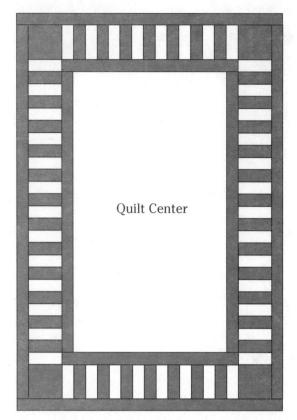

Garden Lattice Assembly Diagram

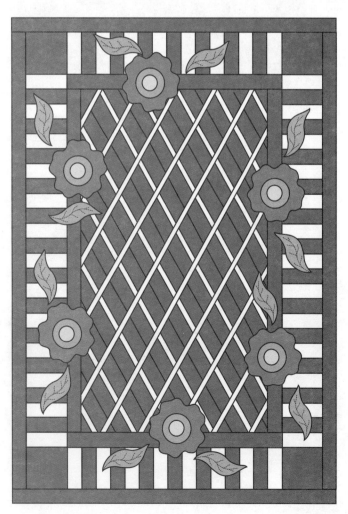

Garden Lattice Finished Assembly Diagram

BORDERS:

Black Border #1:
Cut 2 strips $2\frac{1}{2}$" x $46\frac{1}{2}$" for sides.
Cut 2 strips $2\frac{1}{2}$" x $30\frac{1}{2}$" for top and bottom.
Sew side borders to the quilt. Press.
Sew top and bottom borders to the quilt. Press.

Piano Keys Border #2:
Cut 21 White strips into $2\frac{1}{2}$" x 13" lengths.
Cut 19 Black strips into $2\frac{1}{2}$" x 13" lengths.

Sides:
Sew 13 White and 12 Black strips together
 W-B-W-B-etc. ending in White
 to make a piece 13" x $50\frac{1}{2}$":
Cut the piece in half to make 2 pieces $6\frac{1}{2}$" x $50\frac{1}{2}$".

Top and Bottom:
Sew 8 White and 7 Black strips together
 W-B-W-B-etc. ending in White
 to make a piece 13" x $30\frac{1}{2}$".
Cut the piece in half to make 2 pieces $6\frac{1}{2}$" x $30\frac{1}{2}$".

Corners:
Cut 3 Black strips $2\frac{1}{2}$" x 26".
Sew the strips together to make a piece $6\frac{1}{2}$" x 26".
Cut the strip into 4 squares $6\frac{1}{2}$" x $6\frac{1}{2}$".
Sew a Corner square to each end of the
 top and bottom borders. Press.

Assembly:
Sew side borders to the quilt. Press.
Sew top and bottom borders to the quilt. Press.

Border #3:
Cut 6 Black strips $2\frac{1}{2}$" by the width of fabric.
Sew strips together end to end.
 Cut 2 strips $2\frac{1}{2}$" x $62\frac{1}{2}$" for sides.
 Cut 2 strips $2\frac{1}{2}$" x $46\frac{1}{2}$" for top and bottom.
 Sew side borders to the quilt. Press.
 Sew top and bottom borders to the quilt. Press.

FINISHING:
Applique:
See Basic Instructions.
Cut out pieces using the patterns on pages 26 - 27..
Applique as desired.

Quilting: See Basic Instructions.
Binding: Cut strips $2\frac{1}{2}$" wide.
 Sew strips together end to end to equal 234".
 See Binding Instructions.

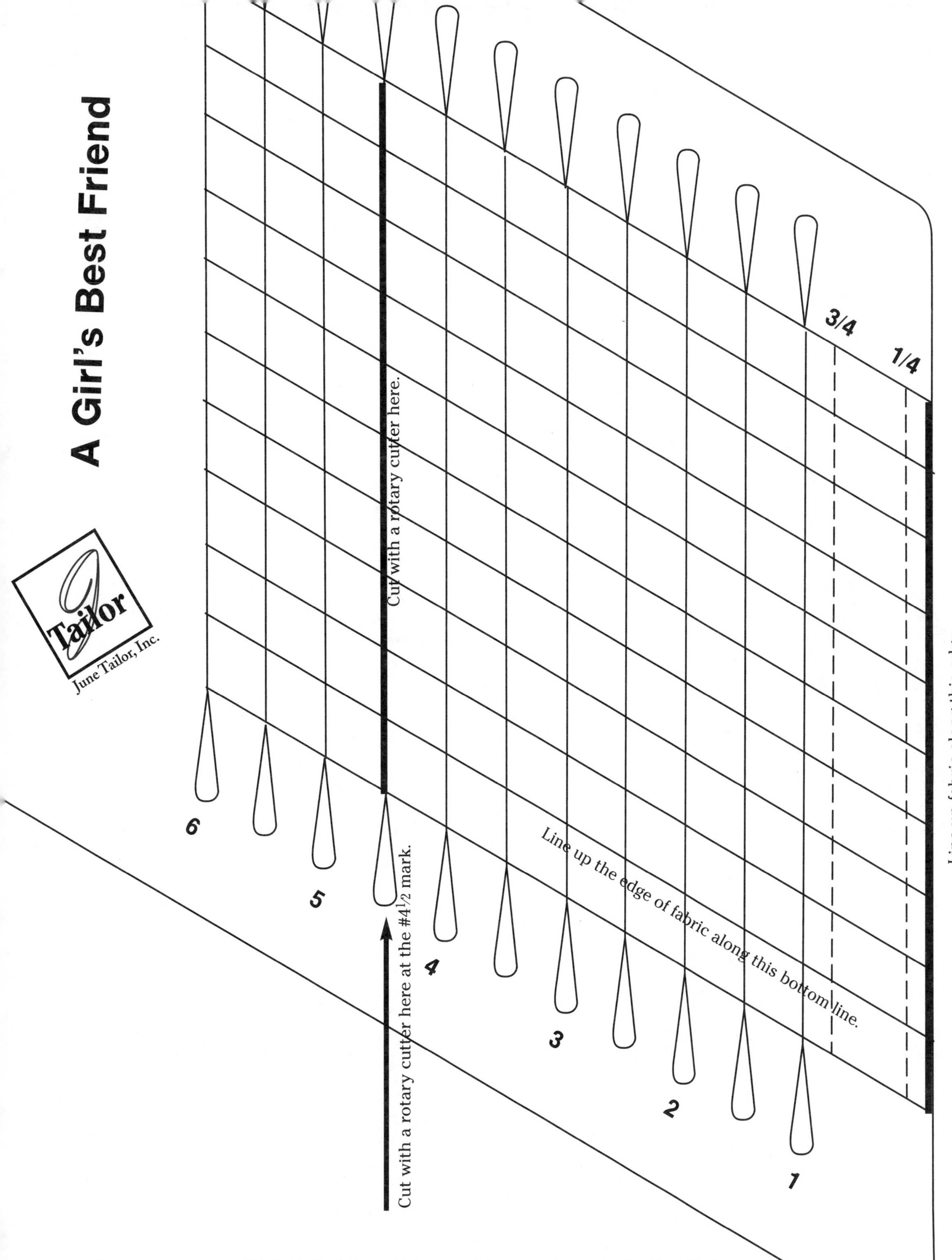

A Girl's Best Friend

June Tailor, Inc.

Cut with a rotary cutter here.

Cut with a rotary cutter here at the #4½ mark.

Line up the edge of fabric along this bottom line.

Line up fabric along this edge

3/4 1/4

6 5 4 3 2 1

Here is a drawing of 'A Girl's Best Friend' Diamond Cut template ruler by *June Tailor*.
This plastic template makes cutting accurate diamonds easy.

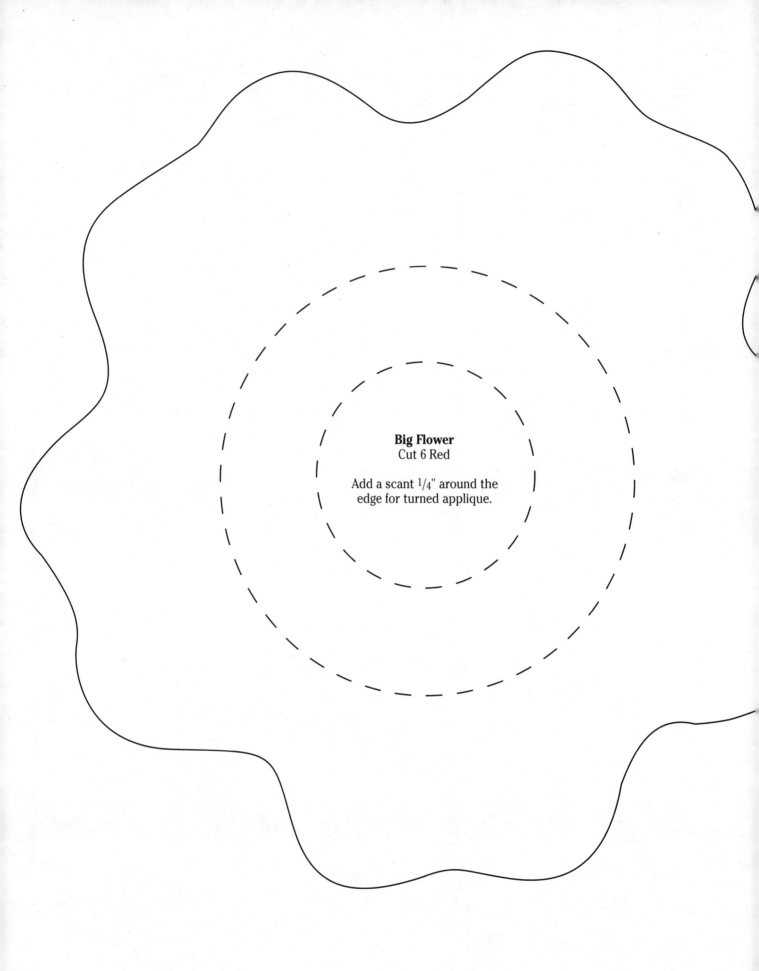

Big Flower
Cut 6 Red

Add a scant $1/4"$ around the
edge for turned applique.

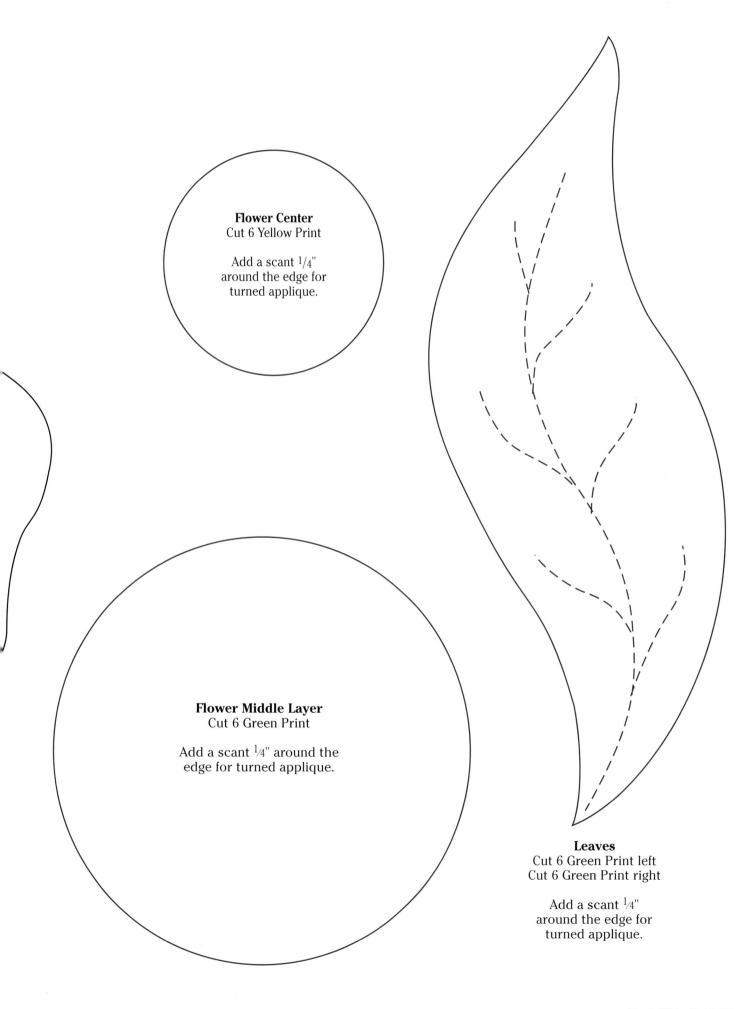

Flower Center
Cut 6 Yellow Print

Add a scant $1/4$"
around the edge for
turned applique.

Flower Middle Layer
Cut 6 Green Print

Add a scant $1/4$" around the
edge for turned applique.

Leaves
Cut 6 Green Print left
Cut 6 Green Print right

Add a scant $1/4$"
around the edge for
turned applique.

Tapestry

photos are on pages 32 - 33.

SIZE: 58" x 78"

YARDAGE:
We used a *Moda* "Basics" Black and a "Basics" White
    'Jelly Roll' collection of $2\frac{1}{2}$" fabric strips
    - we purchased 1 'Jelly Roll' of each

20 strips	OR	$1\frac{1}{2}$ yards of Color A - White
38 strips	OR	$2\frac{2}{3}$ yards of Color B - Black

Blocks and Binding   Purchase $1\frac{3}{8}$ yards of Color C - Black print
Backing   Purchase $4\frac{1}{2}$ yards
Batting   Purchase 66" x 86"
Sewing machine, needle, thread

PREPARATION FOR STRIPS:
    Cut all Black and White strips $2\frac{1}{2}$" by the width
        of fabric (usually 42" - 44").
    Label the stacks or pieces as you cut.

FABRIC FOR BORDERS AND CORNERS OF BLOCKS:
    Color A - White Borders and Corners:
    Cut 12 strips $2\frac{1}{2}$" x $10\frac{1}{2}$" for side borders.
    Cut 12 strips $2\frac{1}{2}$" x $14\frac{1}{2}$" for top and bottom borders.
    Cut 24 squares, each $2\frac{1}{2}$" x $2\frac{1}{2}$" for Snowball Corners.

    Color B - Black Borders and Corners:
    Cut 12 strips $2\frac{1}{2}$" x $14\frac{1}{2}$" for side borders.
    Cut 12 strips $2\frac{1}{2}$" x $18\frac{1}{2}$" for top and bottom borders.

    Cut 4 strips $2\frac{1}{2}$" x 42" for Snowball Corners.
    Sew 2 strips together side by side to make a $4\frac{1}{2}$" wide piece.
        Make 2 sets. Press.
    Cut 24 squares from the strip-sets, each $3\frac{1}{2}$" x $3\frac{1}{2}$".

FABRIC FOR INDIVIDUAL BLOCKS:
Fabric or Scraps for Centers:
    Color C - Black print
    Cut 6 squares, each $10\frac{1}{2}$" x $10\frac{1}{2}$" for Centers.
    Cut 24 squares, each $4\frac{1}{2}$" x $4\frac{1}{2}$" for Snowball Corners.

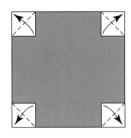

Snowball Corners
To sew blocks refer to this diagram.
Align a square with each corner of a square.
Draw a diagonal line on each corner as shown.
Sew on each line.
Fold the corners back and press.
Repeat for all corners.

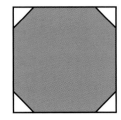

Block Center

SEW BLOCKS:
    Refer to the Block Assembly diagram to make 6 blocks.

Block Center:
    Begin with a $10\frac{1}{2}$" x $10\frac{1}{2}$" Black print square.

White Snowball Corners:
Refer to the Snowball Corner instructions.
    Align a White $2\frac{1}{2}$" square on each corner of the
        center square.
    Sew on the diagonal, fold back and press.

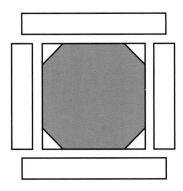

White Border #1:
    Sew a $10\frac{1}{2}$" strip to the right and left sides of each
        center square. Press.
    Sew a $14\frac{1}{2}$" strip to the top and bottom of each
        center square. Press.

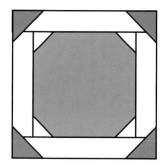

Black Snowball Corners:

Align a Black $3\frac{1}{2}$" x $3\frac{1}{2}$" square on each corner
of the center block.
Sew on the diagonal, fold back and press.

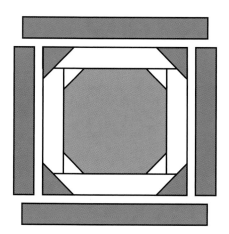

Black Border #2:

Sew a $14\frac{1}{2}$" strip to the right and left sides of each
block. Press.
Sew an $18\frac{1}{2}$" strip to the top and bottom of each
block. Press.

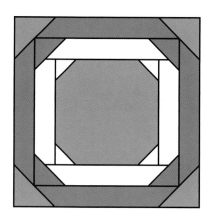

Finished Block

Black print Snowball Corners:

Use 24 squares $4\frac{1}{2}$" x $4\frac{1}{2}$" from Fabric C - Black print.

Align a $4\frac{1}{2}$" x $4\frac{1}{2}$" square on each corner of the
center block.
Sew on the diagonal, fold back and press.
Make a total of 6 center blocks.

FABRIC FOR CHECKERBOARD SASHING:
Sashing:
  Color A - White Fabric for Checkerboard
  Cut 4 strips $2\frac{1}{2}$" x $42\frac{1}{2}$".

  Color B - Black Fabric for Checkerboard
  Cut 5 strips $2\frac{1}{2}$" x $42\frac{1}{2}$".

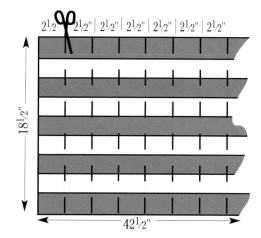

CHECKERBOARD SASHING:

Refer to the Checkerboard diagram above.
Use 5 Black strips $42\frac{1}{2}$" long.
Use 4 White strips $42\frac{1}{2}$" long.
Sew the strips together side by side with
  B-W-B-W etc. ending in Black. Press.

Cut a total of 17 checkeerboard strips $2\frac{1}{2}$" x $18\frac{1}{2}$".

ASSEMBLE THE ROWS:
Cornerstones:
  Color B - Black Fabric
  Cut 12 squares $2\frac{1}{2}$" x $2\frac{1}{2}$".

Assembly:
Arrange all blocks and Sashing strips on a work surface.

Rows 1, 3, 5 & 7:
Sew Cornerstone - Sashing - Cornerstone - Sashing - Cornerstone.
  Press.

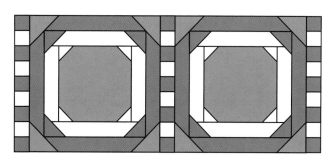

Rows 2, 4 & 6:
Sew Sashing - Block - Sashing - Block - Sashing.
  Press.

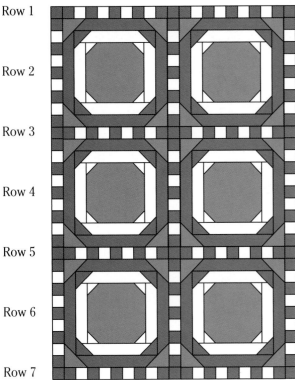

Row 1

Row 2

Row 3

Row 4

Row 5

Row 6

Row 7

Tapestry Quilt
Center Assembly Diagram

ASSEMBLY:
Refer to the Quilt Assembly diagram.

Assembly:
    Sew the rows together. Press.

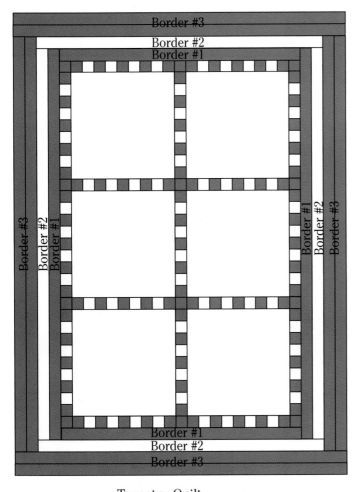

Tapestry Quilt
Border Assembly Diagram

BORDERS:
Border #1:
Sew the Black strips together end to end.
    Cut 2 strips $2\frac{1}{2}$" x $42\frac{1}{2}$" for top and bottom.
    Cut 2 strips $2\frac{1}{2}$" x $66\frac{1}{2}$" for sides.

    Sew top and bottom borders to the quilt. Press.
    Sew side borders to the quilt. Press.

Border #2:
Sew the White strips together end to end.
    Cut 2 strips $2\frac{1}{2}$" x $66\frac{1}{2}$" for sides.
    Cut 2 strips $2\frac{1}{2}$" x $50\frac{1}{2}$" for top and bottom.

    Sew side borders to the quilt. Press.
    Sew top and bottom borders to the quilt. Press.

Border #3:
Sew the Black strips together end to end.
    Cut 4 strips $2\frac{1}{2}$" x $70\frac{1}{2}$" for sides.
    Cut 4 strips $2\frac{1}{2}$" x $54\frac{1}{2}$" for top and bottom.
    Sew 2 side strips together side by side.
        Make 2. Press.
    Sew 2 top & bottom strips together side by side.
        Make 2. Press.

    Sew side borders to the quilt. Press.
    Sew top and bottom borders to the quilt. Press.

Tapestry Quilt
Finished Assembly Diagram

FINISHING:
Quilting:
See Basic Instructions.

Binding:
Cut strips 2½" wide.
Sew together end to end to equal 282".
See Binding Instructions.

Tapestry

pieced by Donna Arends Hansen
quilted by Susan Corbett

Like the keys on a piano, the black and white patterns in this quilt weave a tapestry of harmonious equilibrium that smoothly fits into any decor with its clean lines and inviting open spaces.

Day and night, light and shadow, no matter how you think about this combination, this natural, neutral mix entertains the eye with movement and grace.

instructions on pages 28 - 31